The Art of Energy Seductio.. ...ustering

The

Human Energy Vampire

Within You

The Art of Energy Seduction is a fascinating topic that has caught the attention of many people in recent years. It's a powerful tool that can be used to attract positive energy and repel negative energy. Mastering this art requires a deep understanding of human energy and how it works. One of the most important aspects of this art is learning how to deal with the human energy vampire within you. This vampire feeds on the energy of others, draining them of their vitality and leaving them feeling exhausted and depleted. By mastering the art of energy seduction, you can learn to control this vampire and use its power for good. With practice and dedication, you can become a master of energy seduction, attracting positive energy, and repelling negative energy wherever you go.

Disclaimer

The information and recipes contained in this book are based upon the research and the personal experiences of the author. It's for entertainment purposes only. It is not meant to replace any advice from a health care professional. This book is meant to compliment. The reader is encouraged to use good judgement when applying the information contained and to seek advice from a qualified professional if, and as needed. Professionals should be consulted as needed prior to undertaking any of the actions endorsed herein.

Every attempt has been made to provide accurate, up to date and reliable information. No warranties of any kind are expressed or implied. Readers acknowledge that the author is not engaging in the rendering of legal, financial, medical, or professional advice. By reading this, the reader agrees that under no circumstance the author is not responsible for any loss,

A.L. Childers

your support of the author's rights. All the data, research and references are sited in the back of the book, and it does back up all claims that have been discussed by the author.

All the data, research, footnotes, and references are cited in the back of the book, and it does back up all claims that have been discussed by the author. The internet is a valuable source of information, but unlike printed works, it cannot be relied upon for long-term reference. News articles may be removed from their websites, and data that you have cited may be erased, or the websites may have been terminated. This represents a challenge to authors who want to document the origin of their information.

Dear readers, it is important to take all necessary precautions before undertaking any DIY project. Always follow the instructions and be extra careful when creating your own homemade products. It is never a good idea to stretch yourself too thin. Remember that every fabric or material may react differently to suggested use. While this is a non-toxic and natural way to clean your home, it is always recommended to wear protective gloves and eyewear. Please note that although every effort has been made to provide you with the best possible information, neither the publisher nor the author is responsible for any accidents, injuries, or damage incurred because of tasks performed by readers. The author will not assume any responsibility for personal or property damage resulting from the formulas found in this book. It is important to keep in mind that this book is separate from professional services.

Authors note:

Please note that any reference or resemblance to any person or organization in this book, whether living or dead, existing, or defunct, is purely coincidental.

A note of caution:

Prioritizing your own health and well-being is essential for a fulfilling life. I firmly believe that self-care and personal health empowerment are powerful tools, and that everyone should take the initiative to improve their own understanding. The more knowledge you have, the more control you have over your own health. However, it's important to remember that consulting with a trained medical professional is always necessary in cases of long-standing and undiagnosed symptoms. This book is not intended to replace professional medical judgment but can certainly serve as a valuable supplement to it. Stay informed and vigilant, but always remember to seek professional advice when needed. Please note that the information provided in this book is for educational and entertainment purposes only, and no warranty is given concerning the accuracy of this information. Be smart, be sensible, and prioritize your health by utilizing good common sense. Above all else, be kind and compassionate towards yourself, your body, and your mind.

An entity is different and specific to each individual or item to which it has attached itself. As to alternative forms of medicine or healing, the author of this book has yet to offer any promised outcomes. Some human issues are more profound than cleansing a new home or spiritual entity possession and removal. Therefore, you must understand that this isn't a quick fix for issues that may have gone on in your or someone else's life. Cleansing a new home or spiritual entity possession and removal is not designed as a replacement for traditional psychological and medical treatment or advice, and it is not intended to treat, diagnose, cure, or prevent any disease. There is a difference between entity removal, energy healing, deep-rooted physiological issues, and demonic possession. If you or someone you know seems to have signs of demonic activity, you should contact a priest for counsel and prayer. In addition, with the corporation and aid of a medical professional, they can help you discern if the symptoms have a more natural cause, physiological or physical. A priest can perform exorcisms if no such reasons can be clearly identified or if they seem to be occupied by a spirit. We don't need special authorization to perform deliverance prayers on a person, place, or object, but if it is an exorcism, you must have someone skilled and trained to perform it correctly.

All in all, a spiritual entity possession and entity attachment removal is not something you merely play around with. A demon will eat your lunch and pop that bag right before you.

As befitted in nature and a world that cannot be seen with human eyes, the author is protected by a binding spell of any malicious intent. Any dark or evil force may return to its source, shield my home, health, heart, and mind, as this includes all family, friends, objects, and animals of mine, as we remain free, always safe, and well indeed. You are bound to return to your source with flight; I banish thee with this holy light.

Dear Creator, please grant me your protection from those who attempt to justify evil actions as good and twist truth into lies to achieve their malicious intentions. I ask that you guard me and my loved ones against any forms of deceit and schemes against righteousness. May we be surrounded by the purest vibrations and a sphere of White Light that encompasses every corner, crack, and shelter of our dwellings. Please keep this sphere of White Light free from any negative or harmful energies, especially those of demonic origin. I also request that this sphere of White Light be expanded to cover the space that we always inhabit, ensuring our safety and well-being. Thank you for your guidance and protection.

Chapter 1: Understanding Energy Vampires

The Concept of Energy Vampires

In the realm of human energy dynamics, there exists a phenomenon known as energy vampires. These individuals possess an uncanny ability to drain the life force of those around them, leaving their victims feeling exhausted, depleted, and emotionally drained. This subchapter aims to explore the concept of energy vampires, shedding light on their characteristics, motivations, and techniques while also providing insights on how to effectively protect oneself from their influence.

Energy vampires, as the name suggests, draw energy from others to sustain themselves. They thrive on the emotional and psychological energy of their victims, using various tactics to manipulate and control those around them. They are often skilled at disguising their true intentions, appearing charming and charismatic on the surface. However, beneath this façade lies a desperate need for external validation and power.

Understanding the motivations behind energy vampires is crucial in order to protect oneself from their influence. Many energy vampires suffer from deep-seated insecurities and a fear of being insignificant or unloved. They seek to compensate for these feelings by asserting control over others and draining their energy. By understanding this underlying psychology, individuals can develop strategies to prevent themselves from becoming victims.

While this subchapter is titled "The Concept of Energy Vampires," it is important to note that the intention is not to encourage individuals to become energy vampires themselves. Rather, the focus is on understanding the dynamics at play, in order to safeguard one's own energy and well-being.

To protect oneself from energy vampires, it is essential to establish strong boundaries and cultivate self-awareness. This involves recognizing the signs of energy vampirism, such as feeling consistently drained or manipulated after interactions with certain individuals. By setting clear limits on what one is willing to give and receive in relationships, it becomes easier to deflect the attempts of energy vampires to drain one's vital life force.

Furthermore, practicing self-care and self-love is paramount in warding off the influence of energy vampires. By prioritizing one's own well-being and investing in activities that replenish and uplift, individuals can build a reservoir of positive energy that is less susceptible to depletion.

The concept of energy vampires' sheds light on a complex and often overlooked aspect of human energy dynamics. By understanding their motivations and techniques, individuals can protect themselves from falling victim to their draining influence. Ultimately, the goal is to empower individuals to master their own energy, cultivating a positive and vibrant life force that is impervious to the tactics of energy vampires.

Different Types of Energy Vampires

In our journey to mastering the art of energy seduction, it is important to understand the different types of energy vampires that exist. Energy vampires are individuals who drain our vital life force energy, leaving us feeling depleted, exhausted, and sometimes even emotionally damaged. These individuals have honed their skills in manipulating and feeding off the energy of others, often without their victims even realizing it. By recognizing the various types of energy vampires, we can protect ourselves from their influence and learn how to become one ourselves.

1. The Emotional Vampire: This type of energy vampire thrives on creating drama and chaos in their relationships. They feed off the emotional turmoil they cause in others, sucking out their positive energy and leaving behind negativity and despair. The emotional vampire is skilled at manipulating others with guilt, shame, and fear, constantly draining their victims' emotional resources.

2. The Narcissistic Vampire: These individuals have an insatiable need for attention and admiration. They feed off the admiration and compliments they receive from others, constantly seeking validation and using their charm to manipulate those around them. The narcissistic vampire uses others as a constant source of praise and admiration, leaving their victims feeling empty and unimportant.

3. The Psychic Vampire: This type of energy vampire has a heightened ability to sense and tap into the energy fields of others. They can drain the life force energy of their victims, leaving them feeling weak and fatigued. Psychic vampires often use subtle manipulation techniques to gain access to their victims' energy, leaving them feeling drained and depleted.

4. The Victim Vampire: This energy vampire thrives on playing the victim in every situation. They constantly seek sympathy and attention from others, draining their victims' energy by constantly complaining and seeking validation for their suffering. The victim vampire is skilled at eliciting pity and sympathy from others, leaving them feeling emotionally drained and exhausted.

By understanding the different types of energy vampires, we can protect ourselves from their influence and learn how to become one ourselves. This knowledge is essential in mastering the art of energy seduction. However, it is important to note that using these skills ethically and responsibly is crucial. The purpose of this book is not to encourage manipulation or harm, but rather to empower individuals to recognize and protect themselves from energy vampires while also understanding their own energy potential.

By harnessing our own energy and becoming aware of the tactics used by energy vampires, we can navigate relationships with clarity and confidence. This subchapter will delve deeper into each type of energy vampire, exploring their characteristics, tactics, and ultimately, how to defend against their draining influence.

Identifying Energy Vampires in Your Life

In order to master the art of energy seduction and truly understand the human energy vampire within you, it is essential to first identify the energy vampires in your life. These individuals can drain your vital life force, leaving you feeling exhausted, emotionally depleted, and even physically unwell. This subchapter will provide you with valuable insights and practical tips on recognizing these energy vampires and protecting yourself from their influence.

Recognizing Energy Vampires:

Identifying energy vampires can be challenging, as they often disguise themselves as ordinary people. However, there are certain telltale signs that can help you distinguish them from others. One common characteristic of energy vampires is their constant need for attention and validation. They thrive on the energy they drain from others, often leaving their victims feeling emotionally drained or manipulated.

Another key trait of an energy vampire is their tendency to create drama or conflict. They may frequently engage in gossip, manipulation, or emotionally charged conversations, seeking to elicit a strong emotional response from those around them. Furthermore, energy vampires often exhibit a lack of empathy, showing little regard for the emotional well-being of others.

Protecting Yourself:

Once you have identified an energy vampire in your life, it is crucial to establish healthy boundaries and protect yourself from their influence. Start by becoming more aware of your own energy levels and how you feel after interacting with certain individuals. If you consistently feel drained or negative after spending time with someone, it may be an indication that they are an energy vampire.

Setting clear boundaries is an essential step in protecting your energy. Learn to say no when necessary and avoid getting caught up in their manipulative tactics. Surround yourself with positive, uplifting individuals who support your well-being. Seek out activities and environments that replenish your energy and promote a sense of inner peace.

Recognizing energy vampires in your life is a vital aspect of mastering the art of energy seduction and understanding the human energy vampire within you. By identifying these individuals, you can take proactive steps to protect yourself from their draining influence. Set clear boundaries, surround yourself with positive influences, and prioritize self-care. Remember, taking care of your own energy is essential for your overall well-being and personal growth.

Chapter 2: The Inner Work

Recognizing Your Own Energy Drains

In the pursuit of mastering the art of energy seduction, it is vital to begin by understanding the concept of energy drains and recognizing them within ourselves. As humans, we possess an inherent ability to both emit and absorb energy, and sometimes, unknowingly, we become energy vampires draining the vital life force from those around us. This subchapter aims to guide you through the process of identifying and acknowledging your personal energy drains, thus helping you take the first steps towards transformation and growth.

One of the most common energy drains is negative thinking. Constantly dwelling on pessimistic thoughts or engaging in self-deprecating conversations can exhaust not only your own energy but also that of those who interact with you. Recognizing this pattern is crucial as it enables you to redirect your thoughts towards positivity and cultivate a more uplifting energy that attracts rather than repels.

Another significant energy drain stems from unresolved emotional baggage. Unprocessed emotions such as anger, guilt, or sadness can weigh heavily on your energetic field, dragging you down and affecting your interactions with others. By acknowledging and addressing these emotions, you can unburden yourself and free up the energy needed for personal growth and positive connections.

Furthermore, being overly dependent on external validation is a common energy drain. Seeking constant approval and validation from others can be exhausting for both parties involved. Learning to find inner validation and self-worth is an essential step towards becoming a master of your own energy.

Additionally, engaging in gossip, drama, or negative conversations can drain your energy rapidly. Participating in such activities not only perpetuates negativity but also attracts individuals who thrive on energy vampirism. Recognizing the detrimental effects of these behaviors allows you to consciously choose to engage in more positive and uplifting conversations, thus preserving and nurturing your energy.

Lastly, neglecting self-care and personal boundaries can also drain your energy. Failing to prioritize your own well-being and constantly putting others' needs before your own can leave you depleted and vulnerable to energy vampires. Recognizing the importance of self-care and setting healthy boundaries is crucial for maintaining your energetic balance and protecting yourself from those who may seek to drain your energy.

By consciously acknowledging and addressing these energy drains, you take the first step towards mastering the art of energy seduction. Remember, the path to becoming an energy vampire is not about manipulating or draining others but rather about mastering your own energy, cultivating positivity, and attracting abundance. Embrace the journey and watch as your energy becomes a magnet for all that you desire.

Exploring Your Emotional Triggers

In the enthralling journey of mastering the art of energy seduction, it is imperative to understand the concept of emotional triggers. Our emotions hold immense power over us, and by exploring them, we can tap into a wellspring of energy that will enable us to become the ultimate energy vampires. This subchapter delves into the depths of your emotional triggers, unlocking the key to harnessing their force and manipulating the energies around you.

Emotional triggers are those deep-seated emotional wounds that lie dormant within us, waiting to be awakened. They are the scars from past experiences that have shaped our beliefs, fears, and desires. By identifying and understanding these triggers, we gain the ability to control them, enabling us to manipulate the emotions of others with ease.

To embark on this exploration, we must first confront our own emotional triggers. Self-awareness is the foundation upon which we build our energy seduction prowess. Through introspection and reflection, we can identify the moments when our emotions are most vulnerable, and subsequently, when we are most susceptible to being drained of our own energy.

Once we have identified our own triggers, we can then use this knowledge to master the art of triggering others. By understanding the emotional landscape of those around us, we gain the ability to manipulate their emotions, leading them into a state of vulnerability. This is where the true power of the energy vampire lies - in the ability to draw sustenance from the emotional energy of others.

However, it is crucial to approach this power with responsibility and empathy. The art of energy seduction is not about causing harm or exploiting others; it is about understanding and connecting with the energies that exist within and around us. By exploring our emotional triggers, we develop a deeper understanding of the human psyche, allowing us to forge more meaningful connections and influence others positively.

Exploring your emotional triggers is an essential step in mastering the art of energy seduction. By delving into the depths of your own emotions and understanding them, you gain the power to manipulate the energies around you. Remember, it is imperative to approach this power responsibly and ethically, using it to forge connections and influence others positively. Through this exploration, you will unlock the true potential of the energy vampire within you and become a master of human energy seduction.

Healing Past Wounds and Traumas

In the subchapter "Healing Past Wounds and Traumas," we delve into a crucial aspect of mastering the human energy vampire within you. While our focus may be on understanding and harnessing the power of energy, it is equally important to acknowledge and heal the wounds and traumas that may have shaped our energy patterns.

As human beings, we all carry scars from our past experiences. These wounds can manifest in various ways, affecting our emotional, mental, and physical well-being. However, as energy vampires, it is crucial to recognize that these wounds can also impact our ability to generate and manipulate energy effectively.

One of the first steps towards healing past wounds and traumas is self-awareness. By acknowledging the pain and trauma we have experienced, we can begin to understand how it has influenced our energy patterns. This self-reflection allows us to identify the triggers and patterns that drain our energy and perpetuate negative cycles.

Once we have gained awareness, it is essential to find healthy and effective methods of healing. This could include professional therapy, energy healing practices, or even engaging in creative outlets that allow us to express and process our emotions.

Forgiveness plays a significant role in the healing process. By forgiving ourselves and others for past hurts, we release the energetic attachments that keep us bound to pain. This liberation allows us to cultivate healthy and balanced energy, empowering us to become more effective energy vampires.

Additionally, practicing self-care and self-love is vital in healing past wounds. By prioritizing our own well-being, we create a solid foundation from which to build and manipulate energy. Engaging in activities that nourish our mind, body, and spirit, such as meditation, exercise, and healthy relationships, helps us replenish and rejuvenate our energy reserves.

Healing past wounds and traumas is a journey that requires patience, compassion, and commitment. As energy vampires, it is essential to understand that our ability to harness energy effectively and ethically is intimately connected to our own healing and growth.

By addressing and healing these wounds, we can transform our energy patterns and become more skilled at manipulating energy in a way that benefits both ourselves and those around us. Ultimately, by healing ourselves, we can pave the

way towards a more conscious and empowered
existence as energy vampires.

Chapter 3: Harnessing Your Energy Vampire Potential

Unleashing Your Inner Power

In the realm of human energy dynamics, a fascinating concept has often been misunderstood and underestimated. It is the power within each of us to tap into our own energy reserves to become masters of our own energetic influence. This subchapter, titled "Unleashing Your Inner Power," is dedicated to exploring this concept and guiding you toward harnessing your true potential as an energy vampire.

Contrary to popular belief, being an energy vampire is not about draining others of their life force or manipulating them for personal gain. Instead, it is about understanding and harnessing the energy that flows within us all. By tapping into this energy, we can enhance our personal magnetism, improve our relationships, and elevate our overall quality of life.

The first step towards unleashing your inner power is to cultivate self-awareness. Take the time to understand your own energetic makeup, recognizing the unique qualities and patterns that define you. This awareness will enable you to identify your strengths and weaknesses, allowing you to channel your energy more effectively.

Next, it is essential to develop a deep connection with your inner self. Through practices such as meditation, visualization, and mindfulness, you can tap into the vast reservoirs of energy that lie within. By honing this connection, you will gain a heightened sense of intuition, enabling you to navigate the energetic landscape more adeptly.

As you delve deeper into your journey of self-discovery, it is crucial to explore and refine your energy manipulation techniques. Learn to control and direct your energy flows, using them to influence and inspire those around you. This does not involve coercion or manipulation but rather a genuine desire to uplift and empower others through the positive energy you radiate.

Furthermore, understanding the delicate balance between giving and receiving energy is key.

Cultivate healthy boundaries to protect your own energy reserves while remaining open to the exchange of energy with others. This equilibrium will ensure that you can sustain and replenish your own energy while still positively impacting those around you.

Finally, remember that unleashing your inner power as an energy vampire is not a means to an end but a lifelong journey of growth and self-improvement. Embrace the transformative power of your energy and strive to use it responsibly and ethically. By doing so, you will unlock the true potential within you and become a beacon of positive energy in the world.

"Unleashing Your Inner Power" is an invitation to explore the depths of your energetic being. By cultivating self-awareness, connecting with your inner self, mastering energy manipulation techniques, and maintaining a balanced exchange, you will become an empowered energy vampire. Embrace this journey, and watch as your life and the lives of those around you are forever transformed by the radiant energy you possess.

Tapping into the Universal Energy

In the realm of human energy dynamics, there is a vast and powerful force that exists all around us - the Universal Energy. This energy is the life force that flows through every living being, connecting us to each other and to the universe itself. Understanding and harnessing this energy is the key to becoming a master of the art of energy seduction.

To tap into the Universal Energy, one must first acknowledge its existence and learn how to access it. It is important to note that this energy is available to all, but only those who are dedicated and open-minded enough can truly harness its potential. Through meditation, mindfulness, and the development of intuitive perception, one can begin to tap into this limitless source of power.

The Universal Energy can be channeled and utilized in various ways. For those seeking to become energy vampires, the focus should be on learning how to draw upon this energy from others. This is not about draining the life force of others, but rather about understanding the energetic exchange that occurs between individuals.

One of the most effective techniques to tap into the Universal Energy is by learning to sense and manipulate the energy fields of others. By understanding the subtle cues and vibrations that emanate from individuals, energy vampires can learn to tap into their energy and draw upon it for their own benefit. This can be done through eye contact, body language, and even through the power of suggestion.

It is important to note, however, that becoming an energy vampire should not be taken lightly. This power comes with great responsibility and should be used ethically and responsibly. The intent should always be to empower oneself and others, rather than to manipulate or harm.

To truly master the art of energy seduction, one must also learn to balance the give and take of energy. Just as we draw upon the Universal Energy from others, we must also be willing to give back. This can be done through acts of kindness, compassion, and by sharing our own positive energy with those around us.

Tapping into the Universal Energy is the key to becoming an energy vampire. By understanding and harnessing this powerful force, one can master the art of energy seduction and use it to empower oneself and others. However, it is important to approach this practice with respect and responsibility, always seeking to uplift and empower rather than manipulate or harm.

Developing Psychic Abilities

In the realm of energy seduction, the mastery of psychic abilities is an essential tool for those seeking to tap into the depths of human energy. Psychic abilities, often regarded as mystical and enigmatic, have long fascinated individuals from all walks of life. Whether you are a beginner or have already embarked on the journey of exploring your psychic potential, this subchapter aims to guide you towards unlocking and developing your innate psychic powers.

To truly understand the art of energy seduction and become an adept energy vampire, you must first realize that psychic abilities are not limited to a select few; they are a natural aspect of being human. By tapping into these abilities, you can harness and manipulate the energies that surround you, enhancing your personal power and influencing others in subtle ways.

The first step in developing your psychic abilities is self-awareness. Take the time to understand your own energy and its fluctuations. Meditation and mindfulness practices can help you become attuned to your own subtle energy vibrations, allowing you to recognize the energy of others more keenly. Through regular practice, you can strengthen your intuition and enhance your sensitivity to the energetic realm.

Next, it is crucial to gain knowledge about various psychic modalities. Explore the diverse branches of psychic abilities, such as clairvoyance, telepathy, precognition, and psychometry. Each of these modalities offers unique insights into the human energy field and can help you deepen your understanding of energy seduction.

Furthermore, practice is paramount. Engage in exercises specifically designed to sharpen your psychic skills. These exercises may include visualization, energy scanning, aura reading, and telepathic communication. Regular practice not only hones your abilities but also builds your confidence in utilizing them effectively.

Additionally, seek the guidance of experienced practitioners and mentors who can provide valuable insights and techniques to accelerate your progress. Joining psychic development circles or attending workshops can expose you to a supportive community of like-minded individuals, fostering growth and exchange of knowledge.

Remember, developing psychic abilities is not about controlling or manipulating others against their will. It is about harnessing your own personal power responsibly, with empathy and respect for the energetic boundaries of others. By understanding and mastering your own energy, you can create harmonious connections and influence others positively.

The journey of developing psychic abilities is a transformative one. As you delve deeper into the realm of energy seduction, remember to approach your psychic development with humility, curiosity, and a genuine desire to connect with others on a profound energetic level. Embrace the adventure that lies ahead, and may your psychic abilities guide you toward mastery of the human energy vampire within you.

Chapter 4: Mastering Energy Seduction Techniques

Manipulating Energy Fields

In the fascinating world of human energy dynamics, one can explore the depths of power and influence. This subchapter delves into the art of manipulating energy fields, unraveling the secrets to becoming an energy vampire. By mastering this skill, you will discover how to harness and control the invisible force that surrounds all living beings - energy.

Understanding energy fields is paramount in the journey of becoming an energy vampire. Each individual emits an energy field that encompasses their physical, emotional, and spiritual existence. By learning to manipulate these fields, you can tap into the vast reservoirs of energy that surround you, feeding off the life force of others to enhance your own vitality and influence.

To begin your journey as an energy vampire, it is essential to develop a heightened sense of awareness. Start by observing the energy fields of those around you. Notice the subtle variations in color, intensity, and movement. This will enable you to identify the individuals who possess abundant energy reserves, perfect for your vampiric endeavors.

Once you have honed your observation skills, it's time to learn the art of energy manipulation. Begin by practicing simple techniques such as visualization and intention setting. Visualize yourself drawing energy from your chosen target, envisioning their energy flowing into your own field, revitalizing, and empowering you. By setting clear intentions, you can direct the energy flow to specific areas of your life, amplifying your own desires and goals.

As you progress, explore advanced techniques such as energy transference and manipulation through touch. Develop the ability to absorb energy directly from another person's field through physical contact, leaving them drained and vulnerable while you thrive. This skill can be particularly potent in intimate relationships, where the exchange of energy can be intense and deeply satisfying.

However, it is crucial to approach this path with responsibility and ethical considerations. Becoming an energy vampire should not be about causing harm or manipulating others for personal gain. Instead, it should be a journey of self-mastery and self-awareness, understanding the delicate balance between giving and receiving energy.

Remember, the art of energy seduction is a lifelong practice that requires discipline, integrity, and respect. As you delve deeper into the realm of energy manipulation, never forget the power you hold and the impact it can have on those around you. With great power comes great responsibility, and by mastering the art of energy seduction, you can become a force for positive transformation in both your life and the lives of those you touch.

Creating Emotional Dependency

One of the most powerful techniques in the art of energy seduction is the ability to create emotional dependency. As humans, we are social creatures who crave connection and validation from others. By understanding and harnessing this innate need, you can become an energy vampire and master the art of manipulating others for your own benefit.

Emotional dependency is the process of intentionally cultivating a deep emotional bond with another person, to the point where they become reliant on your presence and validation for their own happiness and self-worth. This technique allows you to tap into their energy reserves and feed off their emotions, effectively turning them into your energetic supply.

To create emotional dependency, you must first establish a strong initial connection with your target. This can be done through charm, charisma, and active listening. By showing genuine interest in their lives and making them feel seen and valued, you lay the foundation for a deep emotional bond.

Once the connection is established, you must gradually increase your presence in their lives. This can be done by offering emotional support, being their confidant, and providing them with a sense of security and stability. By positioning yourself as their go-to person for emotional comfort, you create a sense of reliance that is hard to break.

Another crucial aspect of creating emotional dependency is the manipulation of their self-esteem. By subtly undermining their confidence and self-worth, you can make them doubt their own abilities and believe that they need you to feel whole. This can be achieved through backhanded compliments, comparison, and manipulation of their insecurities.

It is important to note that creating emotional dependency should be done ethically and responsibly. It is crucial to respect the boundaries and consent of others, and never exploit their vulnerability for personal gain. The art of energy seduction is a tool for personal growth and understanding, not a means to harm others.

Creating emotional dependency is a powerful technique in the art of energy seduction. By understanding and harnessing the innate need for connection and validation, you can become an energy vampire and manipulate others for your own benefit. However, it is important to approach this technique ethically and responsibly, always respecting the boundaries and consent of others. The art of energy seduction is a journey of self-discovery and personal growth, allowing you to master the human energy vampire within you.

Influencing Others' Energy Levels

Welcome to the intriguing subchapter on "Influencing Others' Energy Levels" from the book "The Art of Energy Seduction: Mastering the Human Energy Vampire within You." In this section, we will explore the powerful techniques that allow you to become a master of influencing the energy levels of those around you. Whether you aspire to become an energy vampire or simply seek to understand the dynamics of human energy, this chapter will provide you with valuable insights and practical tips.

Understanding Energy Dynamics:

Before delving into the art of influencing others' energy levels, it is essential to comprehend the fundamental principles of human energy. Energy is the life force that flows within us, affecting our emotions, thoughts, and overall well-being. By understanding the ebb and flow of energy, you can tap into the immense power of influencing others and shaping their experiences.

Techniques for Influencing Energy Levels:

1. Harnessing Emotional Resonance: Emotions are contagious, and by consciously projecting desired emotions, you can influence the energy of those around you. Learn to embody and radiate positive emotions such as joy, love, and enthusiasm, creating a magnetic field that draws others towards you.

2. Mirroring and Matching: People naturally feel more comfortable around individuals who mirror their energy and behaviors. By subtly mirroring others' body language, speech patterns, and energy levels, you can establish rapport and gradually influence their energy to align with yours.

3. Active Listening and Empathy: People crave to be heard and understood. By actively listening to others and empathizing with their emotions, you can create a powerful connection that allows you to influence their energy positively. Offer genuine support and understanding to uplift their spirits.

4. Cultivating Charisma: Charisma is the ability to captivate and inspire others. By developing your charisma, you can effortlessly influence the energy levels of those around you. Focus on developing qualities such as confidence, charm, and a positive aura that naturally attracts and energizes others.

5. Setting Boundaries: Energy vampires understand the importance of setting boundaries to protect their own energy while subtly influencing others'. By establishing healthy limits and asserting your needs, you can maintain your energy levels while subtly guiding others to interact with you in a desired manner.

Mastering the art of influencing others' energy levels is a powerful skill that can enhance your relationships, personal growth, and overall well-being. While this subchapter provides valuable insights into the techniques used by energy vampires, it is vital to remember that energy seduction should always be practiced ethically and with respect for others' boundaries. Use these techniques responsibly and consciously, always aiming to uplift and empower those around you.

Chapter 5: Protecting Yourself from Energy Vampires

Establishing Boundaries

In the realm of human interaction, maintaining healthy boundaries is crucial for our overall well-being and energetic balance. This subchapter delves into the art of establishing boundaries, an essential skill for those seeking to navigate the intricate world of energy seduction. Whether you are an individual looking to protect your energy or someone delving into the realm of energy vampirism, understanding, and implementing boundaries is of utmost importance.

Boundaries serve as energetic fences, guarding our inner selves against external influences that may drain our vitality. They act as a shield, allowing us to maintain a healthy level of personal power and prevent others from encroaching upon our energy reserves. For those aspiring to become energy vampires, it is vital to comprehend the delicate balance between giving and taking energy and respect the boundaries of others.

Setting boundaries involves both self-reflection and assertiveness. Begin by recognizing your own needs and limits. Take time to understand what energizes and depletes you and identify situations or individuals that may infringe upon your energetic equilibrium. Once you have gained this self-awareness, communicate your boundaries clearly and assertively to those around you. This is crucial in order to establish mutual understanding and respect.

For individuals aspiring to master the art of energy vampirism, it is essential to approach the establishment of boundaries with caution and empathy. Remember that energy seduction is an intricate dance of power dynamics, and violating another person's boundaries can have severe consequences. Instead, focus on creating an environment of trust and consent. Seek permission from potential energy donors and ensure that they are willing participants in this exchange. By doing so, you not only avoid potential harm but also cultivate healthier and more sustainable relationships.

Furthermore, boundaries are not solely about protecting oneself but also about respecting the boundaries of others. As an energy vampire, it is crucial to be attuned to the signals and cues given by potential energy sources. Recognize when they are reaching their limits and honor their need for space or autonomy. By establishing healthy boundaries for yourself and respecting those of others, you create a harmonious and balanced energy exchange.

Establishing boundaries is an integral part of mastering the art of energy seduction. Whether you are seeking to protect your own energy or delve into the realm of energy vampirism, understanding and implementing boundaries is paramount. Through self-reflection, assertiveness, and empathy, you can create an environment that fosters healthy, energetic exchanges and cultivates sustainable relationships. Remember, true mastery lies in the delicate balance between giving and taking energy while respecting the boundaries of oneself and others.

Shielding Your Energy Field

In the realm of human energy dynamics, we often encounter individuals who drain our vitality and leave us feeling depleted. These energy vampires possess a unique ability to tap into our life force and feed off our energy, leaving us vulnerable and exhausted. However, just as vampires have their weaknesses, so do energy vampires. In this subchapter, we will explore the art of shielding your energy field, empowering you to protect yourself against these energy-draining entities.

Understanding Your Energy Field:

Before delving into shielding techniques, it is crucial to comprehend the concept of your energy field. Every human possesses an energy field, also known as an aura, which surrounds their physical body. This energetic shield acts as a barrier, protecting your life force from external influences. However, energy vampires possess the uncanny ability to infiltrate and manipulate this field, extracting your vital energy for their own benefit.

Recognizing Energy Vampires:

To effectively shield yourself, you must first identify the energy vampires in your life. These individuals often exhibit manipulative behavior, constantly seeking attention, and draining your emotional reserves. By recognizing their tactics, you can take proactive steps to safeguard your energy field and prevent further depletion.

Shielding Techniques:

1. Visualization and Intention: Begin by closing your eyes and envisioning a brilliant, impenetrable shield surrounding your energy field. Intend for this shield to repel any negative or draining energies, allowing only positive and nourishing vibrations to enter.

2. Grounding and Centering: Connect with the Earth's energy by visualizing roots extending from your feet, grounding you firmly into the ground. This practice helps you maintain stability and resilience, making it harder for energy vampires to access your life force.

3. Crystals and Gemstones: Utilize the natural energetic properties of crystals and gemstones to fortify your energy field. Amethyst, black tourmaline, and clear quartz are particularly effective in repelling negative energies and strengthening your aura.

4. Setting Energetic Boundaries: Clearly communicate your boundaries to energy vampires, making it known that you will not tolerate their draining behavior. Reinforce these boundaries by envisioning a force field around you that repels any attempts at intrusion.

Shielding your energy field is essential in protecting yourself from energy vampires who seek to drain your life force. By understanding the nature of your energy field, recognizing these vampires, and utilizing effective shielding techniques, you can regain control over your energy and maintain a balanced and vibrant existence. Remember, the power to shield yourself lies within you - embrace it and reclaim your energetic sovereignty.

Cutting Off Energy Drain Sources

In the pursuit of understanding and mastering the art of energy seduction, it is crucial to recognize the importance of cutting off energy drain sources. This subchapter aims to enlighten you, dear reader, about the detrimental effects of energy vampirism and how to break free from these draining patterns. By taking control of your own energy and empowering yourself, you can lead a more fulfilling and harmonious life.

Understanding Energy Vampirism:

Energy vampirism is a concept that encompasses the idea of individuals who unconsciously or consciously drain the vital life force energy of others. It is a parasitic behavior that can result in emotional exhaustion, physical ailments, and overall imbalance. By recognizing the signs and patterns of energy vampirism, we can effectively address and eliminate these energy drains from our lives.

Identifying Energy Drain Sources:

First and foremost, it is crucial to identify the sources of energy drain in your life. These can manifest in various forms such as toxic relationships, emotional manipulation, excessive social media consumption, or self-destructive habits. By acknowledging and understanding these sources, you can begin the process of cutting them off and reclaiming your energy.

Setting Boundaries:

To become an empowered individual, it is essential to establish healthy boundaries. Boundaries act as protective shields, safeguarding your energy from being drained by others. Learn to say no to excessive demands, prioritize self-care, and surround yourself with individuals who respect and support your boundaries. By doing so, you can create a nurturing environment that promotes positive energy flow.

Cultivating Self-Awareness and Self-Care:

Self-awareness is the key to identifying and addressing energy drain sources effectively.

Engage in regular self-reflection, introspection, and mindfulness practices to better understand your emotional and energetic state. Prioritize self-care activities that recharge and replenish your energy, such as exercise, meditation, or hobbies that bring you joy. By investing in yourself, you create a strong foundation to resist and overcome energy vampires.

Seeking Support:

Remember, you are not alone in this journey. Seek out like-minded individuals who are also striving to break free from energy vampirism. Engage in support groups, workshops, or seek guidance from energy healing practitioners who can offer valuable insights and techniques to protect and strengthen your energy field.

Cutting off energy drain sources is a vital step in mastering the art of energy seduction and liberating yourself from the chains of energy vampirism. By setting boundaries, cultivating self-awareness, and seeking support, you can reclaim your energy, restore balance, and lead a more fulfilling life. Remember, you hold the power to become the master of your own energy, and in doing so, you can inspire and uplift those around you.

Chapter 6: Nurturing Positive Energy

Cultivating Self-Love and Self-Care

Cultivating Self-Love and Self-Care: Nurturing
Your Inner Energy Vampire

In this subchapter, we will take a different
approach to the concept of energy vampires.
Rather than focusing on how to become one, we will
explore the crucial importance of self-love and
self-care in managing and transforming our own
energy. By cultivating a deep sense of self-worth
and nurturing our inner selves, we can harness our
energy in positive ways and create harmonious
relationships with others. Let's delve into the art
of cultivating self-love and self-care, enabling us
to master the human energy vampire within us.

Understanding Self-Love:

Self-love is the foundation for personal growth and
emotional well-being. It involves accepting yourself
unconditionally and recognizing your intrinsic
worth. By practicing self-love, we can develop a
healthy sense of self-esteem, confidence, and
resilience. This newfound self-awareness allows us

to better understand our own energy patterns and how they impact those around us.

Self-Care Practices:

Self-care is the deliberate act of nurturing our physical, mental, and emotional well-being. It involves setting boundaries, prioritizing our needs, and engaging in activities that recharge our energy. By incorporating self-care practices into our daily lives, we can maintain a balanced energetic state and prevent ourselves from becoming energy vampires.

1. Setting Boundaries: Establishing clear boundaries is essential to protect our energy and maintain healthy relationships. Learn to say no when necessary and avoid overextending yourself. This allows you to conserve your energy for the things that truly matter.

2. Prioritizing Emotional Well-being: Embrace activities that promote emotional resilience, such as meditation, journaling, or therapy. By taking care of our emotional health, we become more

attuned to our energy and can consciously direct it towards positive interactions.

3. Physical Health: A healthy body supports a healthy mind and soul. Prioritize exercise, nourishing foods, and adequate rest to optimize your energy levels. Engage in activities that bring you joy and help you connect with your physical self.

Transformation and Connection:

By embracing self-love and self-care, we shift our focus from becoming energy vampires to becoming energy transformers. As we learn to nourish ourselves, we become better able to support and uplift others without depleting our own energy reserves. This transformation empowers us to cultivate deep and meaningful connections based on mutual respect and understanding.

Cultivating self-love and self-care is a transformative journey that allows us to master the human energy vampire within us. By prioritizing our well-being and embracing practices that nourish our mind, body, and soul, we can harness our energy in positive ways. As we develop a strong foundation of self-love, we can form healthy connections and contribute positively to the energy dynamics within our relationships and communities. Remember, your energy is a valuable resource, and by nurturing it, you can create a life filled with love, joy, and fulfillment.

Building Healthy Relationships

In this subchapter, we will explore the importance of building healthy relationships in the context of mastering the human energy vampire within you. While the title of the book might suggest otherwise, it is crucial to understand that the true essence of energy seduction lies in creating mutually beneficial and respectful connections with others.

As humans, we possess an innate desire for companionship and connection. However, it is essential to recognize that healthy relationships are built on a foundation of trust, empathy, and genuine care for one another. The primary goal should never be to become an energy vampire, but rather to develop the skills necessary to navigate relationships with emotional intelligence and understanding.

To begin building healthy relationships, it is crucial to cultivate self-awareness. By understanding our own needs, emotions, and triggers, we can approach interactions with others from a place of authenticity and honesty. This self-awareness enables us to communicate our desires and boundaries effectively, fostering an environment of mutual respect and understanding.

Empathy is another key element in healthy relationships. By putting ourselves in others' shoes, we can gain a deeper understanding of their experiences and emotions. This understanding allows us to respond in a compassionate and supportive manner, strengthening the bond between individuals.

Communication plays a vital role in building healthy relationships. Open and honest communication fosters trust and allows for the expression of thoughts, feelings, and concerns. Effective communication also involves active listening, where we genuinely pay attention to others' words and non-verbal cues, creating a space for meaningful dialogue.

Boundaries are essential in any healthy relationship. By setting clear boundaries, we establish what we are comfortable with and what is not acceptable. Respect for these boundaries ensures that both parties feel safe and valued within the relationship.

Lastly, it is important to cultivate a mindset of mutual growth and support. Healthy relationships are not about power dynamics or draining others' energy. Instead, they should be about uplifting and empowering one another. By encouraging personal growth and celebrating each other's successes, we create an environment where both individuals can thrive.

Building healthy relationships is a fundamental aspect of mastering the human energy vampire within you. By cultivating self-awareness, empathy, effective communication, and respect for boundaries, we can create connections that are nourishing, supportive, and fulfilling. Remember, the art of energy seduction lies not in becoming an energy vampire, but rather in harnessing the power of positive energy to uplift and inspire those around us.

Attracting Abundance and Positivity

Attracting Abundance and Positivity: Unleashing Your Inner Power

Welcome to the subchapter titled "Attracting Abundance and Positivity" from the book "The Art of Energy Seduction: Mastering the Human Energy Vampire Within You." While the title may suggest an exploration into energy vampirism, this subchapter takes a different approach. Here, we focus on harnessing your inner power to attract abundance and positivity, steering away from negative energy and instead embracing a more fulfilling and vibrant life. So, let's dive in and discover the secrets to unlocking your true potential!

1. The Power of Your Energy:

In order to attract abundance and positivity, it is crucial to understand and master the power of your own energy. Your thoughts, emotions, and actions emit vibrations that resonate with the universe. By cultivating a positive mindset and aligning your energy with your desires, you can manifest abundance in all areas of your life.

2. Cultivating a Positive Mindset:

Positive thinking is a catalyst for attracting abundance and positivity. Learn to identify and transform negative thought patterns into empowering beliefs. Practice gratitude, affirmations, and visualization to reprogram your subconscious mind and create a more positive outlook.

3. Embracing Self-Love and Self-Worth:

Attracting abundance starts with self-love and self-worth. When you value and respect yourself, you open the doors for positive opportunities to flow into your life. Prioritize self-care, set healthy boundaries, and surround yourself with people who uplift and inspire you.

4. Aligning with Abundance:

To attract abundance, it is essential to align your energy with abundance itself. Let go of scarcity mentality and embrace an abundance mindset. Practice generosity, embrace the law of attraction, and trust in the universe's infinite possibilities.

5. Embracing Gratitude:

Gratitude is a powerful tool for attracting abundance and positivity. By acknowledging and appreciating the blessings in your life, you invite more to be grateful for. Start a gratitude practice, journal daily, and express gratitude for both big and small things.

6. Taking Inspired Action:

While positive energy is crucial, it must be coupled with inspired action. Set goals, visualize your desired outcomes, and take consistent steps toward achieving them. Embrace opportunities, learn from setbacks, and always believe in your ability to manifest your dreams.

By implementing the principles of attracting abundance and positivity, you can transform your life and tap into your limitless potential. Remember, you have the power to create your reality and manifest the life you desire. Embrace the energy of abundance, cultivate positivity, and watch as your life unfolds in magnificent ways. May your journey be filled with joy, fulfillment, and endless possibilities!

Chapter 7: Balancing Your Energy Exchanges

Giving and Receiving Energy

Giving and Receiving Energy: Nurturing the Art of Energy Seduction

Welcome to the subchapter on "Giving and Receiving Energy" from the book, "The Art of Energy Seduction: Mastering the Human Energy Vampire within You." While the title may intrigue some, this chapter is designed to help you understand the dynamics of energy exchange and how to cultivate healthy energy interactions. Whether you consider yourself a "human" or are interested in exploring the concept of energy vampirism, this chapter will provide valuable insights into the art of giving and receiving energy.

Understanding Energy Exchange:

Energy is an intangible force that connects all living beings. We constantly emit and absorb energy, making it crucial to understand how these exchanges impact our well-being. In energy seduction, it is essential to maintain a balanced flow of energy, ensuring a harmonious and mutually beneficial exchange.

Giving Energy:

When it comes to giving energy, it is crucial to cultivate the art of conscious giving. Offering positive energy with genuine intent can uplift others, inspire them, and foster a harmonious connection. By sharing love, kindness, and compassion, we can positively influence those around us, creating a ripple effect of positivity.

Receiving Energy:

Receiving energy is equally important as giving it. Openness and receptivity allow us to absorb positive energy from our surroundings. By acknowledging and appreciating the energy offered to us, we encourage others to continue sharing their positive vibrations. However, it is essential to be discerning and protect ourselves from any negative energies that may be draining or harmful.

Navigating Energy Vampirism:

While energy vampirism may have a negative connotation, understanding its principles can help us protect our energy and avoid being drained. This chapter offers insights into recognizing energy vampires and provides strategies to set healthy boundaries. By establishing clear limits, we can maintain our energy levels and ensure balanced exchanges.

Cultivating Healthy Energy Interactions:

The art of energy seduction is not about exploiting others for personal gain but rather fostering mutually beneficial relationships. By becoming conscious of our energy exchanges, we can create an environment where everyone benefits, promoting harmony and personal growth.

As we conclude this subchapter on "Giving and Receiving Energy," it is essential to remember that energy seduction is about nurturing positive connections and fostering personal growth. By cultivating a balanced and conscious approach to energy exchange, we can harness the power of energy to uplift ourselves and those around us.

Embracing this art allows us to become masters of our own energy, leading to a more fulfilling and harmonious existence.

Recognizing Healthy Energy Interactions

In the realm of human interactions, energy plays a crucial role. It is the invisible force that connects us, influencing the dynamics of our relationships and shaping our experiences. Understanding and recognizing healthy energy interactions is vital for fostering positive connections and maintaining emotional well-being.

Contrary to popular belief, the purpose of this subchapter is not to encourage you to become an energy vampire, but rather to equip you with the knowledge necessary to identify and avoid such individuals. By recognizing healthy energy interactions, you can safeguard yourself from falling prey to those who seek to drain your vitality.

One of the key aspects of healthy energy interactions is the concept of reciprocity. In a healthy relationship, energy flows freely and harmoniously between individuals. It is a give-and-take dynamic, where both parties contribute and benefit from the exchange. This reciprocity ensures that neither person is left feeling drained or depleted.

Another crucial element is the presence of positive energy. Healthy interactions are characterized by an abundance of positive emotions, such as love, joy, and compassion. These emotions uplift and energize both individuals involved, creating a nurturing and supportive environment.

Furthermore, healthy energy interactions are marked by boundaries and respect. Each person involved understands and respects the personal space and energy of the other. Boundaries act as protective shields, preventing energy vampires from infiltrating and draining your vitality.

To recognize healthy energy interactions, it is essential to cultivate self-awareness. Understanding your own energy levels and emotional states allows you to discern when your energy is being drained and when it is being replenished. Pay attention to how you feel after interacting with certain individuals – do you feel energized and uplifted, or do you feel drained and exhausted?

Lastly, trust your intuition. Your gut feeling is a powerful tool in discerning healthy energy interactions. If something feels off or if your intuition warns you about someone, listen to it. Your intuition is often a reliable guide in navigating the energetic landscape of human interactions.

Recognizing healthy energy interactions is crucial for maintaining emotional well-being and protecting yourself from energy vampires. By understanding the principles of reciprocity, positive energy, boundaries, self-awareness, and intuition, you can cultivate healthy relationships and avoid falling victim to those who seek to drain your energy.

Maintaining a Harmonious Energy Flow

In the realm of energy seduction, it is crucial to
not only understand how to tap into and harness
the energies around you but also to ensure a
harmonious flow that benefits both yourself and
those you interact with. Becoming an energy
vampire is not solely about draining others' energy;
it is about learning to navigate the intricate web of
human energy and creating a synergy that elevates
all parties involved.

To maintain a harmonious energy flow, one must
first recognize the importance of self-awareness.
Understanding your own energy patterns, needs,
and limitations is fundamental. Just as a skilled
painter must know their brushes and colors, an
energy vampire must be intimately acquainted with
their own energetic makeup. This self-awareness
allows you to avoid unnecessary clashes and
imbalances that could disrupt the harmonious
energy flow.

Another crucial aspect is empathy and compassion
towards others. While it may be tempting to solely
focus on extracting energy from those around you,

true mastery lies in creating a reciprocal exchange that leaves everyone involved feeling fulfilled. By being attuned to the needs and emotions of others, you can adapt your energy seduction techniques, accordingly, ensuring a positive and harmonious experience for all parties.

Maintaining a harmonious energy flow also requires a deep understanding of boundaries. As an energy vampire, it is essential to respect the energetic boundaries of others and establish your own. This means recognizing when to withdraw and allow others to recharge, thereby fostering a sustainable and balanced energy exchange. By establishing healthy boundaries, you not only prevent potential conflicts but also create an environment where energy can flow freely and harmoniously.

Furthermore, self-care practices play a vital role in maintaining a harmonious energy flow. Just as a garden requires regular watering and nurturing, your own energy system needs proper attention and care. Engaging in activities that replenish and rejuvenate your energy reserves, such as meditation, exercise, or spending time in nature, allows you to sustain your own energetic harmony, which in turn positively impacts those around you.

Sustaining a harmonious energy flow is an integral part of mastering the art of energy seduction. By cultivating self-awareness, practicing empathy and compassion, setting and respecting boundaries, and prioritizing self-care, you can create a dynamic where energy flows in harmony and elevates everyone involved. Remember, the true power of an energy vampire lies not in draining others but in fostering a mutually beneficial exchange that nurtures and uplifts all.

Chapter 8: Ethical Practices for Energy Vampires

Consenting Energy Exchange

Consenting Energy Exchange: Nurturing Harmonious Connections

In the realm of human energy dynamics, it is crucial to understand that energy exchange is an inherent part of our daily interactions. Each of us possesses the potential to influence and be influenced by the energetic vibrations around us. However, it is essential to approach this concept with responsibility and respect for others. This subchapter delves into the idea of consenting energy exchange, exploring how we can cultivate mutually beneficial connections without crossing ethical boundaries.

1. Recognizing the Power of Energy:

Before embarking on a journey of understanding energy exchange, it is vital to comprehend the immense power it holds. Energy is the life force that flows within us, affecting our emotions, thoughts, and actions. As humans, we can harness this energy to create positive interactions and foster deep connections.

2. The Importance of Consent:

Consenting energy exchange emphasizes the significance of mutual agreement and respect in our energetic interactions. While some may seek to become energy vampires, it is crucial to recognize the ethical boundaries of such practices. Consent ensures that both parties willingly engage in an energy exchange, fostering healthy connections based on trust and understanding.

3. Cultivating Positive Energy:

To engage in a consenting energy exchange, it is imperative to cultivate positive energy within ourselves. This involves nurturing self-awareness, practicing self-care, and developing emotional intelligence. By becoming attuned to our own energy and emotions, we can better navigate interactions with others, ensuring a harmonious exchange.

4. The Art of Energetic Boundaries:

Consenting energy exchange requires us to establish and respect energetic boundaries. It is essential to recognize our limits and communicate them effectively. By setting clear boundaries, we can safeguard our own energy and create an environment that encourages consent in all energetic interactions.

5. The Power of Intention:

Intention plays a pivotal role in energy exchange. By setting positive intentions, we can direct our energy towards uplifting and inspiring others. When both parties have aligned intentions, the energy exchange becomes a catalyst for growth, healing, and personal transformation.

Consenting energy exchange is an art that empowers individuals to create meaningful connections while respecting the energetic boundaries of others. By cultivating positive energy, establishing boundaries, and approaching interactions with clear intentions, we can harness the power of energy exchange for personal and collective growth. Remember, as human beings, we possess the ability to elevate one another through consensual, positive energy exchanges, fostering a world filled with harmony and understanding.

Using Your Powers Responsibly

In our journey towards mastering the art of energy seduction, it is essential to emphasize the importance of using our powers responsibly. Becoming an energy vampire comes with great responsibility, as we wield formidable abilities that can significantly impact the lives of those around us. It is crucial to recognize that our actions can either uplift and empower others or drain and harm them. Therefore, it is imperative that we approach our newfound abilities with mindfulness and empathy.

First and foremost, we must understand that energy seduction is not about manipulation or coercion. It is about cultivating a deep connection with the energy around us and using it to enhance our own lives and the lives of others. When we tap into our energy vampire potential, we must remember to always respect the free will and autonomy of those we interact with. We should never force or impose our will upon others, but rather seek mutually beneficial exchanges of energy.

One of the key principles of responsible energy seduction is consent. Just as in any relationship, we must obtain consent before engaging with another person's energy field. It is essential to be mindful of personal boundaries and to respect the choices of individuals who may not be open to sharing their energy with us. By seeking consent, we establish a foundation of trust and ensure that our interactions are based on mutual understanding and agreement.

Another vital aspect of responsible energy seduction is self-awareness. We must continually reflect on our intentions and motivations, ensuring that they align with ethical principles. It is crucial to regularly assess our own energy levels and emotional well-being, as well as the impact our actions may have on others. By practicing self-awareness, we can recognize when we may be crossing boundaries or exerting undue influence and take steps to correct our behavior.

Moreso responsible energy seduction involves nurturing and uplifting those around us. Rather than solely focusing on our own needs, we should strive to contribute positively to the energy dynamics of our relationships. By enriching the lives of others and helping them tap into their own energetic potential, we create a harmonious and balanced environment that benefits everyone involved.

Becoming an energy vampire is a powerful transformation that requires great responsibility. By using our powers responsibly, we can ensure that our interactions are based on consent, self-awareness, and mutual benefit. Let us embrace the art of energy seduction with integrity and empathy, empowering ourselves and those around us to thrive in a world filled with vibrant energy and connection.

Embracing Empathy and Compassion

Embracing Empathy and Compassion: The Path to Transcending Energy Vampirism

In this subchapter, we will explore a powerful transformational journey that involves embracing empathy and compassion as a means to transcend the energy vampire within you. While the book primarily focuses on understanding energy vampires, it is crucial to recognize the potential for personal growth and positive change that lies within each of us. By cultivating empathy and compassion, you can enhance your relationships, find inner peace, and ultimately become a source of positive energy for others.

Understanding the Destructive Nature of Energy Vampirism:

Energy vampirism refers to the unhealthy habit of draining others' energy for personal gain. However, this behavior is detrimental not only to those being targeted but also to the energy vampire themselves. It creates a cycle of negativity and dissatisfaction, preventing personal growth and fulfillment.

The Power of Empathy:

Empathy is the ability to understand and share the feelings of others. By developing empathy, you can break free from the self-centered mindset that drives energy vampirism. Empathy allows you to genuinely connect with others, acknowledging their emotions and experiences without judgment. Through active listening and seeking to understand, you can forge deeper connections and foster a sense of unity.

Cultivating Compassion:

Compassion goes hand in hand with empathy and involves taking action to alleviate the suffering of others. When you embrace compassion, you shift your focus from self-serving behaviors to acts of kindness and support. By extending a helping hand and showing genuine care, you create a positive ripple effect that benefits both yourself and those around you.

The Transformative Journey:

Embracing empathy and compassion requires self-reflection and a willingness to change. Begin by recognizing the negative patterns and behaviors that contribute to energy vampirism. Engage in mindfulness practices to develop self-awareness and gain insights into your actions and their impact on others. Practice forgiveness, both towards yourself and others, to release any resentment or negative emotions that may fuel energy vampirism.

Becoming a Source of Positive Energy:

By actively nurturing empathy and compassion, you transform into a source of positive energy. This shift not only benefits your relationships but also empowers you to attract genuine connections and experience personal growth. As you radiate positivity, others will be drawn to your authentic and compassionate nature, creating a harmonious and uplifting environment.

Embracing empathy and compassion is a transformative journey that enables you to transcend the energy vampire within you. By cultivating these qualities, you can break free from destructive patterns, foster meaningful connections, and become a source of positive energy for yourself and others. Remember, the art of energy seduction lies not in draining others but in uplifting them and embracing the transformative power of empathy and compassion.

Chapter 9: Embracing Your Authentic Self

Embodying Your True Essence

Embodying Your True Essence: Harnessing Energy Seduction for Personal Growth

Welcome to the subchapter titled "Embodying Your True Essence" from the book "The Art of Energy Seduction: Mastering the Human Energy Vampire within You." While the title might suggest a guide to becoming an energy vampire, this subchapter takes a different approach. Rather than encouraging manipulation or harmful behavior, it explores how understanding and mastering your own energy can lead to personal growth, self-awareness, and positive relationships. So, let's delve into the transformative power of embracing your true essence.

Unleashing Self-Awareness:

To embark on the path of embodying your true essence, self-awareness is paramount. Reflect on your thoughts, emotions, and behaviors to identify any negative patterns or energy imbalances.

Acknowledge the impact of your actions on others and take responsibility for the energy you emit. By understanding your own energetic signature, you can begin to shape it consciously.

Healing and Balance:

Healing past wounds and achieving balance are crucial steps in embodying your true essence. Addressing unresolved traumas, limiting beliefs, and negative self-talk allows you to release stagnant energy and create space for positive transformation. Utilize various techniques like meditation, energy healing, or therapy to facilitate this healing process.

Authenticity and Alignment:

Embodying your true essence requires authenticity and alignment with your core values and desires. Shed societal expectations or the need for external validation to honor your unique self. Embrace your passions, talents, and aspirations, allowing them to guide your life choices and actions. In doing so, you radiate an authentic energy that attracts positivity and like-minded individuals.

Nurturing Healthy Relationships:

As you embrace your true essence, you will naturally attract healthier, more fulfilling relationships. Surround yourself with individuals who uplift, support, and energize you. Learn to set boundaries and protect your energy, ensuring it remains aligned with your intentions and aspirations. Cultivate empathy and compassion, understanding that true connection involves mutual growth and respect.

Harnessing Energy Seduction for Positive Impact:

Now, armed with self-awareness and a strong foundation, you can harness the principles of energy seduction for positive impact. By radiating positive energy, you become a source of inspiration and motivation for others. Share your knowledge, talents, and experiences to uplift those around you, promoting collective growth and transformation.

Embodying your true essence is a profound journey of self-discovery, personal growth, and positive transformation. By mastering your own energy, healing past wounds, and aligning with your authentic self, you can create a life that radiates positivity, attracts healthier relationships, and impacts others in a meaningful way. Embrace the power within you and embark on this transformative path to become the best version of yourself.

Overcoming Fear and Judgment

Overcoming Fear and Judgment: Harnessing Personal Power in The Art of Energy Seduction

In the world of energy seduction, the journey towards mastering your inner energy vampire requires self-reflection, growth, and the ability to overcome fear and judgment. This subchapter delves into the vital aspects of embracing personal power, shedding limiting beliefs, and harnessing your true potential in becoming an energy vampire. Whether you are just starting your journey or seeking to refine your skills, understanding these fundamental principles will empower you to thrive amidst the complexities of human relationships.

1. Embracing Vulnerability:

To truly become an energy vampire, one must first overcome the fear of vulnerability. Recognize that vulnerability is not a weakness, but rather a gateway to authentic connection and personal growth. By embracing vulnerability, you open yourself up to the energy exchanges that fuel your seductive power. Embrace your imperfections, acknowledge your fears, and allow yourself to be seen for who you truly are.

2. Releasing Judgment:

Judgment can hinder your growth as an energy vampire. It stems from insecurities and biases that prevent you from fully embracing the diverse energies around you. Challenge yourself to release judgment and approach each interaction with an open mind. By accepting others for who they are, you create a safe space for energy to flow freely, leading to more meaningful connections.

3. Overcoming Fear:

Fear is an intrinsic part of the human experience, but it should not dictate your journey towards mastering energy seduction. Identify the fears that hold you back and confront them head-on. Whether it is the fear of rejection or the fear of failure, acknowledge its presence and work through it. Overcoming fear will enable you to step into your personal power and radiate the energy that captivates others.

4. Cultivating Self-Confidence:

Confidence is the cornerstone of successful energy seduction. Develop a deep sense of self-awareness, recognizing your strengths and weaknesses. Cultivate self-confidence by nourishing your mind, body, and spirit. Engage in practices such as meditation, positive affirmations, and self-care routines that strengthen your sense of self-worth. Remember, confidence attracts energy, making you an irresistible force in any interaction.

5. Embodying Authenticity:

In the world of energy seduction, authenticity is key. Strive to be true to yourself and honor your unique energy signature. Embodying authenticity allows you to attract and engage with energies that align with your own. Authenticity fosters trust, creating an environment where energy can flow harmoniously, and seduction becomes effortless.

Overcoming fear and judgment is a transformative step towards mastering the art of energy seduction. By embracing vulnerability, releasing judgment, overcoming fear, cultivating self-confidence, and embodying authenticity, you will unlock the immense power within you. Remember, the path to becoming an energy vampire is a lifelong journey of self-discovery and growth. Embrace the challenges, celebrate your progress, and embrace the seductive power that lies within.

Embracing the Power of Vulnerability

Embracing the Power of Vulnerability: A Key to Mastering the Human Energy Vampire Within You

In the fascinating world of energy seduction, where human beings possess the power to influence others and manipulate their energy, it is crucial to understand the importance of embracing vulnerability. Contrary to popular belief, becoming an energy vampire does not solely rely on draining others of their energy, but rather on mastering the delicate balance of vulnerability and strength. In this subchapter, we delve into the transformative power of vulnerability and how it can enhance your journey as an energy vampire.

Understanding Vulnerability:

Vulnerability is often misunderstood as a sign of weakness. However, it is the very essence of our humanity. To become an energy vampire, one must acknowledge and embrace their own vulnerabilities. By accepting our own imperfections, fears, and insecurities, we tap into a deep well of emotional authenticity and connection with others.

Unleashing Authenticity:

Authenticity is the key to unlocking the power of vulnerability. As an energy vampire, you must learn to be genuine and true to yourself, allowing others to see the real you. By acknowledging and expressing your true emotions, desires, and intentions, you create a safe and inviting space for others to share and connect.

Building Trust:

Trust is the foundation of any successful energy vampire. By embracing vulnerability, you demonstrate your willingness to open up and be honest with others. This sincerity builds trust, allowing you to establish strong and lasting connections. Through trust, you gain access to a vast reservoir of energy, which can be harnessed for personal growth and influence.

Creating Emotional Intimacy:

Vulnerability opens the door to deep emotional intimacy. As an energy vampire, your ability to connect with others on a profound level is crucial.

By sharing your vulnerabilities with others, you encourage them to reciprocate, forging a bond built on trust and understanding. This emotional connection enables you to influence and manipulate energy more effectively.

Harnessing Empathy:

Empathy is a powerful tool in the arsenal of any energy vampire. By embracing vulnerability, you cultivate a heightened sense of empathy toward others. Understanding their vulnerabilities and fears allows you to tap into their energy more effortlessly. Empathy also enables you to anticipate their needs, creating a symbiotic relationship where both parties benefit.

In the realm of energy seduction, embracing vulnerability is not a weakness but a strength. By acknowledging and embracing your own vulnerabilities, you gain the ability to connect deeply with others, build trust, and access new sources of energy. Remember, true power lies not in draining others but in fostering authentic connections that elevate both yourself and those around you. Embrace vulnerability as a catalyst for personal growth and mastery of the human energy vampire within you.

Chapter 10: Mastering the Human Energy Vampire Within You

Integrating Your Shadow Self

In the realm of energy seduction, it is essential to understand the concept of integrating your shadow self. While the term "energy vampire" might evoke negative connotations, it is crucial to recognize that everyone possesses both light and dark aspects within themselves. This subchapter delves into the process of embracing and integrating your shadow self, offering guidance on how to become a more balanced and empowered individual.

The shadow self refers to the unconscious aspects of our personality that we often reject or deny. These hidden facets encompass our fears, insecurities, repressed desires, and unresolved traumas. By acknowledging and embracing our shadow self, we gain a deeper understanding of ourselves and harness the full spectrum of our personal power.

To embark on the journey of integrating your shadow self, self-reflection and self-awareness are key. Begin by examining your own thoughts, behaviors, and emotions without judgment. Observe the patterns that emerge and identify the aspects of yourself that you tend to suppress or disown. This process can be uncomfortable, but it is an essential step toward self-growth and transformation.

Once you have identified your shadow aspects, the next step is to acknowledge and accept them. Understand that these aspects are not inherently "bad" or "wrong." They are simply parts of your being that have been neglected or misunderstood. By embracing these shadows, you can begin to integrate them into your conscious awareness.

Shadow integration involves exploring these suppressed parts of yourself and bringing them into the light. Engage in practices such as journaling, therapy, or meditation to delve into the depths of your psyche. By shining a compassionate light on your shadows, you can release their hold on you and reclaim your power.

Integrating your shadow self also involves cultivating self-compassion and forgiveness. Understand that everyone has their own shadows, and acknowledging and accepting them is a part of the human experience. By extending understanding and forgiveness towards yourself, you create a space for growth and healing.

As you integrate your shadow self, you will notice a newfound sense of wholeness and authenticity. Embracing your shadows allows you to tap into a deeper well of personal power and authenticity. You will find that your relationships become more genuine and fulfilling, as you no longer rely on draining others for energy.

Remember, the journey of integrating your shadow self is an ongoing process. It requires continued self-reflection and a commitment to personal growth. By embracing your shadows, you become a more empowered individual, capable of navigating the complex dynamics of energy seduction with grace and authenticity.

Transforming Negative Energy into Positive

In the realm of human energy dynamics, negativity is a force that can consume and drain us, leaving us feeling depleted and dispirited. However, what if we could harness this negative energy and transform it into a positive force within ourselves? This subchapter explores the art of converting negative energy into positive, empowering individuals to become masters of their own energy.

To begin this transformation, it is essential to understand the root causes of negativity. Negative energy often stems from unresolved emotions, past traumas, or unhealthy thought patterns. By acknowledging these sources, we can start the process of healing and release. Engaging in self-reflection, therapy, or energy healing practices such as meditation or Reiki can help in this regard.

Once we have identified and addressed the underlying causes of negativity, it is time to shift our focus towards cultivating positive energy. One of the most effective ways to do this is through gratitude. Gratitude has a profound impact on our energy, allowing us to shift our perspective and appreciate the blessings in our lives. By practicing gratitude daily, we train our minds to seek out the positive aspects of any situation, thereby transforming negative energy into positive vibrations.

Another potent method for transforming negative energy is through self-care and self-love. Nurturing ourselves physically, emotionally, and spiritually replenishes our energy reserves, making it easier to counteract negativity. Engaging in activities that bring us joy, setting healthy boundaries, and prioritizing self-care rituals such as exercise, healthy eating, and mindfulness practices are crucial steps in this transformative process.

Moreover, surrounding ourselves with positive individuals and creating a supportive environment also contributes to this positive energy shift. Building a network of like-minded individuals who uplift and inspire us strengthens our own positive energy reserves and shields us from external negativity.

Ultimately, the transformation of negative energy into positive is a continual process. It requires self-awareness, dedication, and an unwavering commitment to personal growth. By mastering this art, we become the architects of our own energy, able to navigate life's challenges with grace and resilience.

Transforming negative energy into positive is a transformative journey that empowers individuals to become masters of their own energy. Through practices such as gratitude, self-care, and cultivating a positive environment, we can harness the power of negativity and transmute it into a force that fuels our growth and resilience. By embarking on this path, we unlock our true potential and become beacons of positive energy in a world that often seeks to sap our vitality.

Embracing Your Role as an Energy Vampire

In this subchapter, we will explore the concept of embracing your role as an energy vampire, delving into the intricacies of how to become one and harnessing the power it holds. Before we begin, it is essential to understand that being an energy vampire does not equate to being a malevolent or destructive force. Instead, it is about recognizing and utilizing the energy within you to create positive change and influence in your life.

To truly embrace your role as an energy vampire, you must first acknowledge and accept the existence of this inherent energy within yourself. Every human has the potential to tap into this energy and channel it for various purposes. However, becoming an energy vampire requires a conscious effort to understand and master this power.

One of the fundamental steps in becoming an energy vampire is self-awareness. This involves recognizing your energy patterns, understanding how you interact with others, and identifying the sources from which you draw energy. By understanding these dynamics, you can begin to consciously direct and manipulate energy to your advantage.

Another crucial aspect of embracing your role as an energy vampire is learning to manage and control your energy exchanges. Energy vampires feed on the life force of others, drawing upon their energy to replenish their own. However, it is essential to do so responsibly and ethically, ensuring that you do not drain others excessively or harmfully.

Furthermore, developing empathy and emotional intelligence is vital for an energy vampire. By understanding the emotions and needs of those around you, you can navigate energy exchanges more effectively. This enables you to establish healthy boundaries, manage your own energy levels, and avoid becoming overwhelmed or drained by external influences.

Embracing your role as an energy vampire also requires a commitment to personal growth and self-improvement. By continuously honing your skills, expanding your knowledge, and exploring different energy practices such as meditation or energy healing, you can enhance your abilities as an energy vampire. This will allow you to have a more significant impact on your own life and the lives of those around you.

Embracing your role as an energy vampire is not about exploiting others or causing harm. It is about recognizing and harnessing the energy within you to create positive change and influence. By understanding the dynamics of energy exchanges, developing empathy, and committing to personal growth, you can become a master of your own energy and contribute to the betterment of yourself and those around you.

Conclusion: Embracing Your Energy Vampire Identity

In the final chapter of "The Art of Energy Seduction: Mastering the Human Energy Vampire within You," we arrive at a crucial juncture in your journey toward self-discovery and empowerment. It is time to embrace your energy vampire identity and fully understand the power that lies within you.

Throughout this book, we have explored the concept of energy vampires, individuals who possess the ability to tap into and manipulate the energy of others. We have delved into the various types of energy vampires and their characteristics, ranging from the emotional vampire to the psychic vampire. But now, it is time to focus on you and how you can harness this extraordinary gift for personal growth and transformation.

By now, you have gained a comprehensive understanding of the dynamics of energy exchanges and the impact they have on your relationships and overall well-being. You have learned to recognize the signs of energy depletion and how to protect yourself from energy vampires who may drain your vitality. However, it is equally vital to acknowledge and embrace your own energy vampire identity.

Embracing your energy vampire identity does not mean becoming a parasitic force, preying on others for personal gain. Instead, it entails recognizing and harnessing your unique abilities to cultivate positive energy exchanges with those around you. By understanding your own energy patterns and needs, you can engage in conscious interactions that promote mutual growth and well-being.

To become a proficient energy vampire, it is crucial to nurture self-awareness and emotional intelligence. By mastering your emotions and understanding how they affect your energy levels, you can better regulate your interactions with others. Additionally, practicing empathy and compassion will enable you to connect deeply with others, fostering healthy energy exchanges that leave both parties feeling uplifted and rejuvenated.

Remember, being an energy vampire is not about dominance or control but rather about creating harmonious energy dynamics. By understanding and embracing your energy vampire identity, you can tap into your full potential and contribute positively to the world around you.

In conclusion, "The Art of Energy Seduction" has equipped you with the knowledge and tools to navigate the intricate world of energy exchanges. By embracing your energy vampire identity, you can harness your unique abilities to create profound connections and make a positive impact on those you encounter. Remember, your energy is a precious resource, and by mastering the art of energy seduction, you can lead a fulfilling and empowered life.

References:

http://www.worldallergy.org/professional/allergic_diseases_center/ige/

http://acaai.org/allergies/types/food-allergy

https://kidshealth.org/en/parents/birth-defects.html

(1)The author would like to thank Valentine Seymour for the research work that Valentine Seymour did on The Human-Nature Relationship and Its Impact on Health: A Critical Review

(2)1Department of Civil, Environmental and Geomatic Engineering, University College London, London, UK

(3)https://www.ncbi.nlm.nih.gov/pmc/articles/PMC5114301/

1. Guiney MS, Oberhauser KS. Conservation volunteer's connection to nature. Ecoposychology (2009) 1(4):187-97.10.1089/eco.2009.0030 [CrossRef]

2. Nisbet EK, Zelenski JM. The NR-6: a new brief measure of nature-relatedness. Front Psychol (2013) 4:813.10.3389/fpsyg.2013.00813 [PMC free article] [PubMed] [CrossRef]

3. Davis JL, Green JD, Reed A. Interdependence with the environment: commitment, interconnectedness, and environmental behaviour. J Environ Psychol (2009) 29:173–80.10.1016/j.jenvp.2008.11.001 [CrossRef]

4. Kaplan R, Kaplan S. The Experience of Nature. Massachusetts: Cambridge University Press; (1989).

5. Hardin G. The tragedy of the commons. Science (1968) 162(3859):1243–8.10.1126/science.162.3859.1243 [PubMed] [CrossRef]

6. Foster JB. The Four Laws of Ecology and the Four Anti-Ecological Laws of Capitalism. New York: Monthly Review Press; (2012).

7. Louv R. Last Child in the Woods: Saving Children from Nature-Deficit Disorder. Chapel Hill, NC: Agonquin Books; (2005).

8. Park BJ, Tsunetsugu Y, Kasetani T, Kagawa T, Miyazaki Y. The physiological effects of Shinrin-yoku (taking in the forest atmosphere or forest bathing): evidence from field experiments in 24 forests across Japan. Environ Health Prev Med (2010) 15:18–26.10.1007/s12199-009-0086-9 [PMC free article] [PubMed] [CrossRef]

9. Ryan CO, Browning WD, Clancy JO, Andrews SL, Kallianparkar NB. Biophilic design patterns: emerging nature-based parameters for health and wellbeing in the built environment. Int J Arch Res (2014) 8(2):62–76.

10. Thompson Coon KJ, Boddy K, Stein K, Whear R, Barton J, Depledge MH. Does participating in physical activity in outdoor natural environments have a greater effect on physical and mental wellbeing than physical activity indoors? A systematic review. Environ Sci Technol (2011) 45(5):1761–2.10.1021/es102947t [PubMed] [CrossRef]

11. Blum HL. Planning for Health: Developmental Application of Social Change Theory. New York: Human Sciences Press; (1974).

12. Hancock T, Perkins F. The Mandala of Health: a conceptual model and teaching tool. Health Educ (1985) 24:8–10.

13. Max-Neef MA. Human Scale Development: Conception, Application and Further Reflections. London: The Apex Press; (1992).

14. Hancock T. Health, human development and the community ecosystem: three ecological models.

Health Promot Int (1993) 8:41–6.10.1093/heapro/8.1.41 [CrossRef]

15. Zinsstag J, Mackenzie JS, Jeggo M, Heymann DC, Patz JA, Daszak P. Mainstreaming One Health. Ecohealth (2012) 9:107–10.10.1007/s10393-012-0772-8 [PMC free article] [PubMed] [CrossRef]

16. Brofenbrenner U. Developmental ecology through space and time: a future perspective. In: Moen P, Elder GH, Luscher K, editors. , editors. Examining Lives in Context: Perspectives on the Ecology of Human Development. Washington, DC: American Psychology Association; (1995). p. 619–47.

17. VanLeeuwen JA, Waltner-Toews D, Abernathy T, Smit B. Evolving models of human health toward and ecosystem context. Ecosyst Health (1999) 5(3):204–19.10.1046/j.1526-0992.1999.09931.x [CrossRef]

18. Wolf M. Is there really such a thing as "One Health"? Thinking about a more than human world from the perspective of cultural anthropology. Soc Sci Med (2014) 129:5–11.10.1016/j.socscimed.2014.06.018 [PubMed] [CrossRef]

19. Min B, Allen-Scott LK, Buntain B. Transdisciplinary research for complex One Health issues: a scoping review of key concepts. Prev Vet Med (2013) 112:222–9.10.1016/j.prevetmed.2013.09.010 [PubMed] [CrossRef]

20. Darwin C. On the Origin of Species by Means of Natural Selection. London: John Murray; (1859).

21. Badyaev AV. Origin of the fittest: link between the emergent variation and biology evolutionary change as a critical question in evolutionary biology. Proc Soc Biol (2011) 278:1921–9.10.1098/rspb.2011.0548 [PMC free article] [PubMed] [CrossRef]

22. Karrenberg S. Speciation genetics: limits and promises. Taxon (2010) 59(5):1404–12.10.2307/20774037 [CrossRef]

23. Noble D. Physiology is rocking the foundations of evolutionary biology. Exp Physiol (2013) 98:1235–43.10.1113/expphysiol.2012.071134 [PubMed] [CrossRef]

24. Sharov AA. Evolutionary constraints or opportunities? Biosystems (2014) 123:9–18.10.1016/j.biosystems.2014.06.004 [PubMed] [CrossRef]

25. Lumsden CJ, Wilson EO. Theory of gene-culture coevolution. Proc Natl Acad Sci U S A (1980) 77:4382–6.10.1073/pnas.77.7.4382 [PMC free article] [PubMed] [CrossRef]

26. Cavalli-Sforza LL, Feldman MW. Cultural Transmission and Evolution: A Quantitative Approach. Princeton: Princeton University Press; (1981). [PubMed]

27. Boyd R, Richerson PJ. Culture and the Evolutionary Process. Chicago: University of Chicago Press; (1988).

28. Cohen MN, Armelagos GJ. Paleopathology at the Origins of Agriculture. Florida: University Press of Florida; (1984).

29. Laland KN, Odling-Smee J, Myles S. How culture shaped the human genome: bringing genetic and human sciences together. Nat Rev (2010) 11:137–45.10.1038/nrg2734 [PubMed] [CrossRef]

30. Bloomfield SF, Stanwell-Smith R, Crevel RWR, Pickup J. Too clean, or not too clean: the hygiene hypothesis and home hygiene. Clin Exp Allergy (2006) 36:402–25.10.1111/j.1365-2222.2006.02463.x [PMC free article] [PubMed] [CrossRef]

31. Gual MA, Norgaard RB. Bridging ecological and social systems coevolution: a review and proposal. Ecol Econ (2010) 69(4):707–17.10.1016/j.ecolecon.2008.07.020 [CrossRef]

32. Simon HA. The behavioral and social sciences. Sci Centennial Issue (1980) 209(4452):72–8. [PubMed]

33. Nelson RR. Evolutionary social science and universal Darwinism. J Evol Econ (2006) 16:491–510.10.1007/s00191-006-0025-5 [CrossRef]

34. Carrera-Bastos P, Fontes-Villalba M, O'Keefe JH, Lindeberg S, Cordain L. The western diet and lifestyle and diseases of civilization. Res Rep Clin Cardiol (2011) 2:15–33.10.2147/RRCC.S16919 [CrossRef]

35. Powell R. The future of human evolution. Br J Philos Sci (2012) 63:145–75.10.1093/bjps/axr027 [CrossRef]

36. Cosmides L, Tooby J. Cognitive adaptations for social exchange. In: Barkow J, Cosmides L, Tooby J, editors. , editors. The Adapted Mind. New York: Oxford University Press; (1992). p. 163–228.

37. Buss DW. How can evolutionary psychology successfully explain personality and individual differences? Perspect Psychol Sci (1995)

4(4):359–66.10.1111/j.1745-6924.2009.01138.x
[PubMed] [CrossRef]

38. Ploeger A, van der Maas HLJ, Raijmakers EJ. Is evolutionary psychology a metatheory for psychology? A discussion of four major issues in psychology from an evolutionary developmental perspective. Psychol Inq (2008) 19:1–18.10.1080/10478400701774006 [CrossRef]

39. Bolhuios JJ, Brown GR, Richardson RC, Laland KN. Darwin in mind: new opportunities for evolutionary psychology. PLoS Biol (2011) 9(7):e1001109.10.1371/journal.pbio.1001109 [PMC free article] [PubMed] [CrossRef]

40. Naess A. The shallow and the deep, long-range ecology movement: a summary. Inquiry (1973) 16:95–100.10.1080/00201747308601682 [CrossRef]

41. Pyle RM. The extinction of experience. Horticulture (1978) 56:64–7.

42. Schultz PW. Assessing the structure of environmental concern: concern for the self, other people, and the biosphere. J Environ Psychol (2001) 21:327–39.10.1006/jevp.2001.0227 [CrossRef]

43. Mayer FS, Frantz CM. The connectedness to nature scale: a measure of individuals' feeling in

community with nature. J Environ Psychol (2004) 24:503-15.10.1016/j.jenvp.2004.10.001 [CrossRef]

44. Wilson EO. Biophilia. Cambridge: Harvard University Press; (1984).

45. Howell AJ, Dopko RL, Passmore HA, Buro K. Nature connectedness: associations with well-being and mindfulness. Pers Individ Dif (2011) 51:166–71.10.1016/j.paid.2011.03.037 [CrossRef]

46. Ulrich RS. View from a window may influence recovery from surgery. Science (1984) 224(4647):420-1.10.1126/science.6143402 [PubMed] [CrossRef]

47. Barton J, Pretty J. What is the best dose of nature and green exercise for improving mental health? A multi-study analysis. Environ Sci Technol (2010) 44:3947-55.10.1021/es903183r [PubMed] [CrossRef]

48. Gullone E. The Biophilia hypothesis and life in the 21st century: increasing mental health or increasing pathology? J Happiness Stud (2000) 1:293-321.10.1023/A:1010043827986 [CrossRef]

49. Depledge MH, Stone RJ, Bird WJ. Can natural and virtual environments be used to promote improved human health and wellbeing? Environ Sci

Technol (2011) 45:4660–5.10.1021/es103907m [PubMed] [CrossRef]

50. Joye Y, van den Berg A. Is love for green in our genes? A critical analysis of evolutionary assumptions in restorative environments research. Urban For Urban Green (2011) 10(4):261–8.10.1016/j.ufug.2011.07.004 [CrossRef]

51. Orr DW. Love it or lose it: the Biophilia revolution. In: Kellert SR, Wilson EO, editors. , editors. The Biophilia Hypothesis. Washington, DC: Island Press; (1993). p. 415–40.

52. Tuan Y-F. Topophilia: A Study of Environmental Perception, Attitudes and Values. Columbia: Columbia University Press; (1974).

53. Ashford R. Socio-economics: an overview. Coll Law Faculty Scholarship (2007) 14:1–6.10.2139/ssrn.882751 [CrossRef]

54. Stedman RC. Is it really just a social construction? The contribution of the physical environment to Sense of lace. Soc Nat Resour (2003) 16:671–85.10.1080/08941920309189 [CrossRef]

55. Relph EC. Place and Placelessness. California: Pion Limited; (1976).

56. Hay R. Becoming ecosynchronous, part 1: the root causes of our unsustainable way of life. Sustain Dev (2005) 13:311-25.10.1002/sd.256 [CrossRef]

57. Glacken CJ. Traces on the Rhodian Shore: Nature and Culture in Western Thought from Ancient Times to the End of the Eighteenth Century. Berkley: University of California Press; (1967).

58. O'Brien E. Human values and their role in the development of forestry policy in Britain. Forestry (2003) 76:3-17.10.1093/forestry/76.1.3 [CrossRef]

59. Liu J, Dietz T, Carpenter SR, Alberti M, Folke C, Moran E, et al. Complexity of coupled human and natural systems. Science (2007) 317:1513-6.10.1126/science.1144004 [PubMed] [CrossRef]

60. Buckeridge JS. The ongoing evolution of humanness: perspectives from Darwin to de Chardin. S Afr J Sci (2009) 105:427-31.

61. Small B, Jollands J. Technology and ecological economics: promethean technology, Pandorian potential. Ecol Econ (2006) 56:343-58.10.1016/j.ecolecon.2005.09.013 [CrossRef]

62. Hardin G. Extensions of "The tragedy of the commons". Science (1998) 280(5364):682–3.10.1126/science.280.5364.682 [CrossRef]

63. Pellow DN. Environmental inequality formation: toward a theory of environmental injustice. Am Behav Sci (2000) 43:581–601.10.1177/00027642000043004004 [CrossRef]

64. Brulle RJ, Pellow DN. Environmental injustice: human health and environmental inequalities. Annu Rev Public Health (2006) 27:3.1–3.22.10.1146/annurev.publhealth.27.021405.102124 [PubMed] [CrossRef]

65. Van Vugt M. Averting the tragedy of the commons: using social psychological science to protect the environment. Curr Dir Psychol Sci (2009) 18(3):169–73.10.1111/j.1467-8721.2009.01630.x [CrossRef]

66. Ostrom E. Coping with tragedies of the commons. Annu Rev Polit Sci (Palo Alto) (1999) 2:493–535.10.1146/annurev.polisci.2.1.493 [CrossRef]

67. Slocombe DA. Environmentalism: a modern synthesis. Environmentalist (1980) 4:281–5.10.1016/S0251-1088(84)92432-X [CrossRef]

68. Mulihill PR. Endless paradox: environmentalism in transition. Futures (2009) 41:502–6.10.1016/j.futures.2009.01.003 [CrossRef]

69. Radkau J. Nature and power: an intimate and ambiguous connection. Soc Sci Hist (2013) 37(3):325–45.10.1215/01455532-2209402 [CrossRef]

70. Foucault M. The Order of Discourse. London: Picador; (1981).

71. Richards JF. The Unending Frontier: An Environmental History of the Early Modern World. Berkeley: University of California Press; (2003).

72. Bahn PG, Flenley JR. Easter Island, Earth Island. New York: Thames and Hudson; (1991).

73. Diamond JM. Collapse: How Societies Choose to Fail or Succeed. New York: Viking; (2005).

74. Hunt TL, Lipo CP. Late colonization of Easter Island. Science (2006) 311(5767):1603–6.10.1126/science.1121879 [PubMed] [CrossRef]

75. Radkau J. Nature and Power: A Global History of the Environment. New York: Cambridge University Press; (2008).

76. Turner JC. Explaining the nature of power: a three-process theory. Eur J Soc Psychol (2005) 35:1–22.10.1002/ejsp.244 [CrossRef]

77. Whited TL. Nature and power through multiple lenses. Soc Sci Hist (2013) 37(3):347–59.10.1215/01455532-2209411 [CrossRef]

78. Lovelock JE. Gaia: as seen through the atmosphere. Atmos Environ (1972) 6:579.10.1016/0004-6981(72)90076-5 [CrossRef]

79. World Commission on Environment and Development. Our Common Future: Report of the World Commission on Environment and Development. Oxford: Oxford University Press; (1987).

80. Hodder K, Bullock J. Nature without nurture? Planet Earth (2005) Winter:30–1.

81. Tidball KG. Urgent Biophilia: human-nature interactions and biological attractions in disaster resilience. Ecol Soc (2012) 17(2):1–18.10.5751/ES-04596-170205 [CrossRef]

82. Adger WN, Dessai S, Goulden M, Hulme M, Lorenzoni I, Nelson DR, et al. Are there social limits to adaptation to climate change? Climate Change (2009) 93:335–54.10.1007/s10584-008-9520-z [CrossRef]

83. Huber M, Knottnerus JA, Green L, van der Horst H, Jadad AR, Kromhout D, et al. How should we define health? BMJ (2011) 343:d4163.10.1136/bmj.d4163 [PubMed] [CrossRef]

84. Saracci R. The World Health Organisation needs to reconsider its definition. BMJ (1997) 314:1409-10.10.1136/bmj.314.7091.1409 [PMC free article] [PubMed] [CrossRef]

85. Cameron E, Mathers J, Parry J. Health and well-being: questioning the use of health concepts in public health policy practice. Crit Public Health (2006) 16(4):347-54.10.1080/09581590601128166 [CrossRef]

86. Kamberi A. Towards a new understanding of health. Alban Med J (2015) 3:114-8.

87. Fleuret S, Atkinson S. Wellbeing, health and geography: a critical review and research agenda. N Z Geog (2007) 63:106-18.10.1111/j.1745-7939.2007.00093.x [CrossRef]

88. Seligman MEP. Positive psychology: an introduction. Am Psychol (2000) 55(1):5-14.10.1037/0003-066X.55.1.5 [PubMed] [CrossRef]

89. Linley PA, Joseph S, Harrington S, Wood AM. Positive psychology: past, present, and (possible)

future. J Posit Psychol (2006) 1(1):3–16.10.1080/17439760500372796 [CrossRef]

90. Seligman MEP. Positive health. Appl Psychol Int Rev (2008) 57:3–18.10.1111/j.1464-0597.2008.00351.x [CrossRef]

91. Donaldson SI, Dollwet M, Rao MA. Happiness, excellence, and optimal human functioning revisited: examining the peer-reviewed literature linked to positive psychology. J Posit Psychol (2015) 10(3):185–95.10.1080/17439760.2014.943801 [CrossRef]

92. Park N, Peterson C, Szvarca D, Vander Molen RJ, Kim ES, Collon K. Positive psychology and physical health: research and applications. Am J Lifestyle Med (2016) 10(3):200–6.10.1177/1559827614550277 [PMC free article] [PubMed] [CrossRef]

93. Ortega FB, Ruiz JR, Castillo MJ, Sjöström M. Physical fitness in childhood and adolescence: a powerful marker of health. Int J Obes (Lond) (2008) 32:1–11.10.1038/sj.ijo.0803774 [PubMed] [CrossRef]

94. Westerterp KR. Assessment of physical activity: a critical appraisal. Eur J Physiol (2009)

105:823–8.10.1007/s00421-009-1000-2 [PubMed] [CrossRef]

95. Tennant R, Hiller L, Fishwick R, Platt S, Joseph S, Weich S, et al. The Warwick-Edinburgh Mental Well-Being Scale (WEMWBS): development and UK validation. Health Qual Life Outcomes (2007) 5(63):1–13.10.1186/1477-7525-5-63 [PMC free article] [PubMed] [CrossRef]

96. Nisbet EK, Zelenski JM, Murphy SA. Happiness is in our nature: exploring 954 nature relatedness as a contributor to subjective well-being. J Happiness Stud (2011) 12:303–22.10.1007/s10902-010-9197-7 [CrossRef]

97. Ziersch AM, Baum FE, MacDougall C, Putland C. Neighbourhood life and social capital: the implications for health. Soc Sci Med (2005) 60:71–86.10.1016/j.socscimed.2004.04.027 [PubMed] [CrossRef]

98. Miles L. Physical activity and health. Br Nutr Found Nutr Health Bull (2007) 32:314–63.10.1111/j.1467-3010.2007.00668.x [CrossRef]

99. Heerwagen J. Biophilia, health and well-being. In: Campbell L, Wiesen A, editors. , editors. Restorative Commons: Creating Health and Well-

Being through Urban Landscapes. Washington, DC: USADA Forest Services; (2009). p. 38–57.

100. Figueiro MG, Rea MS, Stevens RG, Rea AC. Daylight and productivity – a possible link to circadian regulation. Proceedings of Light and Human Health: EPRI/LRO 5th International Lighting Research Symposium, 2002 Nov 3-5; Palo Alto, CA. and Ostram Sylvania, Danvers, MA California: EPRI (2004).

101. Boyce PR. The impact of light in buildings on human health. Indoor Built Environ (2010) 19(1):8–20.10.1177/1420326X09358028 [CrossRef]

102. Chevalier G, Sinatra ST, Oschman JL, Sokal K, Sokal P. Earthing: health implications of reconnecting the human body to the earth's surface electrons. J Environ Public Health (2012) 2012:291541.10.1155/2012/291541 [PMC free article] [PubMed] [CrossRef]

103. White MP, Alcock I, Wheeler BW, Depledge MH. Would you be happier living in a greener urban area? A fixed effects analysis of panel data. Psychol Sci (2012) 24(6):920–8.10.1177/0956797612464659 [PubMed] [CrossRef]

104. UK Department of Health. Evidence gaps and current/ongoing research. A Compendium of Factsheets: Wellbeing across the Life Course. London: UK Department of Health; (2014).

105. Grinde B, Patil GG. Biophilia: does visual contact with nature impact on health and well-being? Int J Environ Res Public Health (2009) 6:2332–43.10.3390/ijerph6092332 [PMC free article] [PubMed] [CrossRef]

106. Fisher JA. The value of natural sounds. J Aesthet Educ (1999) 33(3):26–42.10.2307/3333700 [CrossRef]

107. Taylor AF, Kuo FE, Sullivan WC. Coping with ADD: the surprising connection to green play settings. Environ Behav (2001) 33(1):54–77.10.1177/00139160121972864 [CrossRef]

108. Luniak M. Synurbization – adaptation of animal wildlife to urban development. Proceedings of the 4th International Symposium on Urban Wildlife Conservation, 876 May 1-5, 1999, Tuscan, Arizona Tuscan: University of Arizona (2004).

109. Burton P, Goodlad R, Croft J. How would we know what works? Context and complexity in the evaluation of community involvement. Evaluation

(2006) 12(3):294–312.10.1177/1356389006069136 [CrossRef]

110. Maas J, van Dillen SME, Verheij RA, Groenewegen PP. Social contacts as a possible mechanism behind the relation between green space and health. Health Place (2009) 15(2):586–95.10.1016/j.healthplace.2008.09.006 [PubMed] [CrossRef]

111. Coley RL, Sullivan WC, Kuo FE. Where does community grow? The social context created by nature in urban public housing. Environ Behav (1997) 29:468–94.10.1177/001391659702900402 [CrossRef]

112. Sullivan WC, Kuo FE, DePooter SF. The fruit of urban nature: vital neighbourhood spaces. Environ Behav (2004) 36(5):678–700.10.1177/0193841X04264945 [CrossRef]

113. Peters K, Elands B, Buijs A. Social interactions in urban parks: stimulating social cohesion? Urban For Urban Green (2010) 9:93–100.10.1016/j.ufug.2009.11.003 [CrossRef]

114. Jones L, Wells K. Strategies for academic and clinician engagement in community-participatory partnered research. JAMA (2007) 24/31:407–10.10.1001/jama.297.4.407 [PubMed] [CrossRef]

115. Tulloch AIT, Possingham HP, Joseph LN, Szabo J, Martin TG. Realising the full potential of citizen science monitoring programs. Biol Conserv (2013) 165:128–38.10.1016/j.biocon.2013.05.025 [CrossRef]

116. Bird W. Our UK natural health service. Socialmedicinsk Tidskrift (2012) 89(3):296–304.

117. Malik VS, Willett WC, Hu FB. Global obesity: trends, risk factors and policy implications. Nat Rev Endocrinol (2013) 9(1):13–27.10.1038/nrendo.2012.199 [PubMed] [CrossRef]

118. Sallis JF, Floyd MF, Rodríguez DA, Saelens BE. Role of built environments in physical activity, obesity, and cardiovascular disease. Circulation (2012) 125:729–37.10.1161/CIRCULATIONAHA.110.969022 [PMC free article] [PubMed] [CrossRef]

119. Stuckler D. Population causes and consequences of leading chronic diseases: a comparative analysis of prevailing explanations. Milbank Q (2008) 86(2):273–326.10.1111/j.1468-0009.2008.00522.x [PMC free article] [PubMed] [CrossRef]

120. Premack D, Premack J. Increased eating in rats deprived of running. J Exp Anal Behav (1963)

6(2):209–12.10.1901/jeab.1963.6-209 [PMC free article] [PubMed] [CrossRef]

121. Frankham R, Loebel DA. Modelling problems in conservation genetics using captive Drosophila populations: rapid genetic adaptation to captivity. Zool Biol (1992) 11:333–42.10.1002/zoo.1430110505 [CrossRef]

122. Bechard A, Lewis M. Modelling restricted repetitive behaviour in animals. Autism (2012) S1:006.10.4172/2165-7890.S1-006 [CrossRef]

123. Depledge MH. Does the pharmaceutical industries need a new prescription? Sci Parliament (2011) 68(4):44–5.

124. Baum FE, Bégin M, Houweling TAJ, Taylor S. Changes not for the fainthearted: reorienting health care systems towards health equity through action on the social determinants of health. Am J Public Health (2009) 99(11):1967–74.10.2105/AJPH.2008.154856 [PMC free article] [PubMed] [CrossRef]

125. Marmot M. Social determinants of health inequities. Lancet (2005) 365:1099–104.10.1016/S0140-6736(05)74234-3 [PubMed] [CrossRef]

126. Navarro V. What we mean by social determinants of health. Int J Health Serv (2009) 39(3):423–41.10.2190/HS.39.3.a [PubMed] [CrossRef]

127. Marmot M, Allen J. Prioritizing health equity. In: Leppo K, Ollila E, Peña S, Wismar M, Cook S, editors. , editors. Health in All Policies: Seizing Opportunities, Implementing Policies. Finland: Ministry and Social Affairs and Health; (2013). p. 63–80.

128. Wolch JR, Byrne J, Newell JP. Urban green space, public health, and environmental justice: the challenge of making cities 'just green enough'. Landscape Plan (2014) 125:234–44.10.1016/j.landurbplan.2014.01.017 [CrossRef]

129. Clark NE, Lovell R, Wheeler BW, Higgins S, Depledge MH, Norris K. Biodiversity, cultural pathways, and human health: a framework. Trends Ecol Evol (2014) 29:198–204.10.1016/j.tree.2014.01.009 [PubMed] [CrossRef]

130. Guerry AD, Polasky S, Lubchenco J, Chaplin-Kramer R, Daily GC, Griffin R, et al. Natural capital and ecosystem services informing decisions: from promise to practice. Proc Natl Acad Sci U S A

(2015) 112(24):7348–55.10.1073/pnas.1503751112 [PMC free article] [PubMed] [CrossRef]

131. Bennett EM, Cramer W, Begossi A, Cundill G, Díaz S, Egoh BN, et al. Linking biodiversity, ecosystem services, and human well-being: three challenges for designing research for sustainability. Curr Opin Environ Sustain (2015) 14:76–85.10.1016/j.cosust.2015.03.007 [CrossRef]

132. Brofenbrenner U, Morris PA. The bioecological model of human development. In: Damon W, Lerner RM, editors. , editors. Handbook of Child Psychology: Theoretical Models of Human Development. London: John Wiley & Sons; (2007). p. 793–828.

133. Prout A. The Future if Childhood. London: Routledge Falmer; (2005).

134. Conn C. Autism and the Social World of Childhood: A Sociocultural Perspective on Theory and Practice. Oxon: Routledge; (2014).

135. Hinchliffe S. More than one world, more than One Health: re-configuring interspecies health. Soc Sci Med (2014) 129:28–35.10.1016/j.socscimed.2014.07.007 [PubMed] [CrossRef]

136. Baird M. Woman Jogging in the Grass Photograph [Online]. (2014). Available from: www.bairdphotos.com

137. Onwuegbuzie AJ, Leech NL. On becoming a pragmatic researcher: the importance of combining quantitative and qualitative research methodologies. Int J Soc Res Methodol (2005) 8(5):375–87.10.1080/13645570500402447 [CrossRef]

138. Onwuegbuzie AJ, Johnson B. Mixed methods research: a research paradigm whose time has come. Educ Res (2006) 33(7):14–26.

139. Tashakkori A, Teddlie C. Validity issues in mixed methods research: calling for an integrative framework. Education Research in the Public Interest, April 7–11, San Francisco, CA. Washington, DC: American Educational Research Association; (2006).

140. https://www.webmd.com/women/features/will-you-inherit-mothers-health-problems#1

141 https://www.nfed.org/learn/genetics-inheritance/

https://beyondpesticides.org/assets/media/docum ents/antibacterial/triclosan-research-3-

09.pdfhttp://blog.earthmamaangelbaby.com/does-castile-soap-kill-germs/

https://www.ncbi.nlm.nih.gov/pmc/articles/PMC2819418/

https://www.ncbi.nlm.nih.gov/pmc/articles/PMC2515351/

https://www.mindbodygreen.com/0-24663/9-lifestyle-changes-i-always-recommend-to-patients-with-autoimmune-diseases.html

https://draxe.com/digestive-enzymes/

https://draxe.com/recipe/beef-bone-broth/

https://www.ncbi.nlm.nih.gov/pubmed/22109896

http://www.ewg.org/tap-water/

http://www.who.int/mediacentre/factsheets/fs313/en/

http://www.who.int/ceh/capacity/Pesticides.pdf

https://www.ncbi.nlm.nih.gov/pmc/articles/PMC2665673/

http://whfoods.org/genpage.php?tname=dailytip&dbid=337

http://sleepfoundation.org/how-sleep-works/how-much-sleep-do-we-really-need

↑ http://www.mayoclinic.org/healthy-lifestyle/adult-health/expert-

Printed in Great Britain
by Amazon

30490740R00079